Pulled & R

..Understanding the Sacrifice, Posture and Benefit of Service

BY
Dabo Davies

Published By
Kratos Publisher

ACKNOWLEDGEMENT

I have been fortunate to serve under some very passionate, humble, dedicated, intelligent and, above all, God-fearing personalities whilst carrying their assignments here on earth. My journey to date is a combination of the tutoring and wisdom received from the Holy Spirit and what I have been taught, directly and indirectly, by these great people.

I am forever grateful to these countless exceptional people who, by their commitment and devotion to becoming the best they could be, have inspired me to do the same. I am grateful for every way they stretched me and, in hindsight, wish they pushed me even more, only if I had understood the importance of the stretch earlier in my life.

I am ever mindful of my precious family's unmatched love, prayer, support, and patience.

To my church family and my countless partners, who, through their love and passion, have become instruments of encouragement, I thank you.

CONTENT

Questions And Answers

INTRODUCTION

"And if you have not been faithful with what belongs to

someone else, who will give you what belongs to you?"

-Jesus Christ (4 B.C.)

Brilliant stage performances create an atmosphere of wonder and awe-inspiring beauty. Think about the lovely melodies, ordered rhythm, and soothing air of precision that envelop the audience and glue everyone to their seats. You can almost reach out to touch the symphony and feel the vibrations that spread throughout the arena. Such unparalleled perfection! Like the glory of an artist in the spotlight, life has its glory at various levels of influence and power.

However, without the pain of preparation, a magnificent performance will remain a dream of the night or a mirage on a sunny day.

For glory, a multitude of people seeks leadership status and influential positions.

They crave the taste of wealth, the fragrance of fame, and the promise of power. There's no mystery to the glory on the stage of life's performance; instinctively, we know that tremendous effort needs to go before the outstanding performance. Just like the minstrel on the guitar, the guitar itself must be pulled and stretched before it can release unique vibrations that create magical melodies.

No guitar ever makes a sound without a release of its strings. The quality and weight of the sound produced are dependent on the effort and expertise employed by the minstrel when the taut string is pulled.

We are all artists on the stage of life and wonder instruments in the hand of our creator. Every man and woman are released and ushered into glory by the providence of God and the force of life's pull.

Hence the springs of gut-level questions: "Are you tucked between the crowds that place preparation on a back burner while masking a temporary success?"

"Have you thought about flourishing in life's performance stage?

Do you feel the need to snap out of irresponsibility to take control of your life?" This book is for you!

Your Life's Heyday

"But we have this treasure in earthen vessels..."

-2 Corinthians 4:7

The truth is that God has put a sound on your inside. This divine note embodies the healing ointment for the wound of nations. It'll interest you to know that from the beginning of the world, God has fit up your life as journals of glory days. He created you to express His beauty through the reverberating sound of deliverance, healing, and an abundance of solution notes installed within you.

Essentially, God fashioned you as an indication of His glorification. He yearns for you to radiate His beauty by taking you through the training route.

There's no escaping the terrain of preparation for you to voice that inner gifting, talent, or skill. In God's agenda, you must grow into a character capable of your destiny. How Ready Are You?

"The creation waits with eager longing for the revealing of the sons of God."

-Romans 8:19

Your Creator delights in you! He loaded you with manifold wonders to save the dying world, and you must rise to the challenge. But first, you must be willing to go through the pulling process. God has some elements in place for you to operate in your appointed reality. Although this climb up the ladder of responsibility might not seem pleasing, it's what you require to become who you were ordained to be. In this book, I referred to these discomforts as the PULLS you must experience before you attain your various heights of release.

Rest assured that your release will come at the right time when you encounter a pull. As you overcome the pain of preparation, you'll realize that your life's transformation has occurred. It'll happen beyond your wildest dreams. And here's the thing: you don't have to leave the training ground.

Instead, be armed with the consciousness that your diligence in service sets you up for unprecedented manifestation. It initiates a revelation of glory manifest through you!

In other words, the extent of your stretch gives room for unreserved release! The writer of the proverbs provides clarity on this thought in Proverbs 22:29:

"Observe people who are good at their work— skilled workers are always in demand and admired; they don't take a backseat to anyone."

- The Message Translation

Are you ready to accept the painful pull that'll launch you into life's spotlight?

The Cards that You're Dealt

Everyone is born with a unique set of passion and personal experiences differing from others. Like a stack of cards, you're dealt with personal experiences to tackle life's game. Your card shades might not necessarily resemble any other person's or what you anticipated.

You might come face to face with ups or lay at the down's end as you go. Now, when the not-so-good moments come, these unprecedented moments are blessings in disguise.

Problems often allow us to display our abilities if they are perceived correctly. A problem is your chance to do your best; growth bounces immediately! The valley situation reveals the strength we have within us, even to our astonishment.

Indeed, embracing the unique training we have been assigned will amplify our sound when the time for the release comes.

We need to let go of our ego and pride as we unashamedly throw ourselves at the blessings of service.

Why is that? It's because, most times, God will not necessarily obliterate the enemy, but He'd instead work on you. Essentially, what we consider an enemy may not go away, but we may have to grow in and through it.

The problem isn't always the enemy but the negative instalments that have glossed our minds. That's why the Scripture recommends in Romans 12:2, *"Do not be conformed to this world, but be transformed by the renewal of your mind, that by testing you may discern what is the will of God, what is good and acceptable and perfect."*

Some of our most significant victories will come not by the destruction of what we think we're fighting against outside our life. But instead, through a change in perspective, how we choose to perceive what we are fighting.

And that may cause an introspection. It will allow us to examine ourselves and find purpose in the fight rather than focus on the fight as a problem.

A change of perspective will determine we evaluate problems.

When you engage life's *PULL* through God's Spirit, you will reap blessings in your *RELEASE*. (Matt 4: 1-11) He'll strengthen you while on the training ground until the point of release, and you'd be free to express yourself and be available to impact your world.

Within the leaves of this book, you'll discover how to rise to outstanding leadership. I'll walk you through the various chapters spotting the microscope on how to survive the hard times while climbing up to power and influence. You'll realize that true fulfilment is tied to your *RELEASE*.

THE HARP

1 Samuel 16:14-23 - New King James Version

14 But the Spirit of the Lord departed from Saul, and a distressing spirit from the Lord troubled him.

15 And Saul's servants said to him, "Surely, a distressing spirit from God is troubling you.

16 Let our master now command your servants, who are before you, to seek out a man who is a skillful player on the harp. And it shall be that he will play it with his hand when the distressing spirit from God is upon you, and you shall be well."

17 So, Saul said to his servants, "Provide me now a man who can play well, and bring him to me."

18 Then one of the servants answered and said, "Look, I have seen a son of Jesse the Bethlehemite, who is skilful in playing, a mighty man of valor, a man of war, prudent in speech, and a handsome person; and the Lord is with him."

19 Therefore, Saul sent messengers to Jesse, and said, "Send me your son David, who is with the sheep."

20 And Jesse took a donkey loaded with bread, a skin of wine, and a young goat, and sent them by his son David to Saul.

21 So David came to Saul and stood before him. And he loved him greatly, and he became his armorbearer.

22 Then Saul sent to Jesse, saying, "Please let David stand before me, for he has found favor in my sight."

23 And so it was, whenever the spirit from God was upon Saul, that David would take a harp and play it with his hand. Then Saul would become refreshed and well, and the distressing spirit would depart from him.

For particular emphasis, I draw our attention to verses 16 and 23 and highlight the instrument *'HARP'.*

16 Let our master now command your servants, who are before you, to seek out a man who is a skillful player on the harp. And it shall be that he will play it with his hand when the distressing spirit from God is upon you, and you shall be well."

23 *And so it was, whenever the spirit from God was upon Saul, that David would take a harp and play it with his hand. Then Saul would become refreshed and well, and the distressing spirit would depart from him.*

Harp – This instrument is called Kinnowr in Hebrew and is from an unused root word meaning - *'Twang.'*

Twang means to give out a sharp, vibrating sound as the strings of a musical instrument are plucked.

It also means a strong ringing sound, such as that made by the plucked string of a musical instrument or a released bowstring:

Therefore, if you twang something such as a tight string or elastic, it makes a reasonably loud, ringing sound because it has been PULLED and then RELEASED.

Contrarywise; the instrument will not produce that vibrating sound if it is not pulled, although it has the potential to do so.

I had an encounter one day and heard the Spirit of the Lord say, for you to be able to release the sound that brings deliverance, healing, raise the dead, and initiate a new move of His glory, you must first be pulled.

I initially did not fully comprehend the depth of this word and what this pull entails until He started bringing clarity, which I will share through this book.

For us to establish national transformation, start a revival and begin a reformation within and outside the four walls of the church, God must first pull us.

The message of the pull becomes essential as we are in a generation where instant gratification is replacing sustainable growth and lasting impact.

People want it now, do me now, bless me now, give me now, appoint me now, showcase me now, announce me now, and we don't want to get trained, get corrected, get rebuked.

We want validation without verification.

We want to be announced but need to be authenticated first.

We want a celebration without certification.

We want to be trusted without being tested, but that's not how God operates.

We don't want to be told; you must play that note again; you have to do it again.

Often there's a need for a restart, but we don't like being told you're not ready yet.

We don't want to be instructed to sit and learn, sit and serve, sit and do some work. But we want to lead.

We don't want to be pulled, but we want to be released.

Even the disciples had to be instructed by Jesus to refrain from engaging in any activity until they were endued with power.

Luke 24:49 - The Living Bible

49 "And now I will send the Holy Spirit upon you, just as my Father promised. Don't begin telling others yet—STAY HERE in the city until the Holy Spirit comes and fills you with power from heaven."

I can imagine how tempting it would have been for the disciples to preach, telling everyone about Jesus; after all, that's a good thing, right? But the instruction was to stay in the city until the Holy Spirit came and filled them with power.

Attempting to preach without the infilling of the Holy Spirit is like trying to be released without being pulled.

Yes, you want to preach, but can you sit for a while?

Sitting in the city may imply submitting to training, discipline, learning, etc. It is a humbling experience that produces power.

Jesus' instruction was explicit, *"don't begin telling others yet"*.

His instruction seems contrary to what we would have considered the correct order of events to tell everyone about Him, to announce to the world the magnificence of our God.

But the lack of understanding of when a thing should be done causes it to be considered less valuable.

Suppose we bring this consideration to our lives. Could some of what God has shown us or given us have appeared to be less impactful and meaningful because we didn't discern the right time?

By implication, the problem wasn't that what God gave us was insignificant or that the place of implementation wasn't correct. It was because we beat the gun. We didn't work according to God's timing. We couldn't humble ourselves to wait.

We must realise that often inactivity is not a sign of a lack of vision or the motivation to work.

It could mean a reliance on God, faith in His process and total dependency on His divine timing, which is all part of the pull.

There must be a PULL before a RELEASE.

Let's see what the pull means:

Pull: According to the dictionary, when you pull something or someone, you hold it *firmly and use force* in order to *move it toward* you or *away from its previous position.*

For some, to be released correctly according to the purpose of God for our lives, we must be forcefully moved from where we are, from who we are with, and from what we are doing.

And sometimes the pull will draw us towards something, someone and someplace we initially would not want to be.

I remember in 2012, before we started the church plant, I intended to travel to the United States to sit under the ministry of a global church leader with the plan of submitting my ministry under his able and well-structured leadership.

But God had another plan. God used a dear pastor friend from Nigeria to give me a timely word. The instruction was to read a book written by another pastor, which led me to visit Ukraine and be mentored by someone I initially wouldn't listen to.

I state this fact because I told this pastor when I met him in Ukraine that I had never listened to him, I don't follow him, and as a matter of fact, he wasn't my kind of preacher. You know, we all have our 'kind of preacher'. And he laughed out loud. But he understood what I said. He was very humble and welcoming, but his training approach was rigorous. We learnt till late and had to wake up early to submit our coursework. It felt like a military camp, but that was what I needed for where I was going.

But the point is, I obeyed God, travelled and sat under this pastor's teaching and training as God instructed in a country I had no intention of travelling to. I had to be there at that time to be where I am today. This period literally began an entire shift in my faith walk.

Some of us are not where we should be because we resisted the pull.

We short-changed our destinies because of temporary comfort and human applause. We chose to bask in the glory of now rather than investing and immersing ourselves in the plan of God, which sometimes includes discomfort for the prize ahead.

My pastor friend introduced me to reading the book, followed by the statement, *'you must build according to the pattern'*. I didn't initially understand clearly what he meant, but in retrospect, what he said implied I would build something I never saw anyone build – I would be pulled in directions I never anticipated.

I don't know if he also understood the complexity of his statement, but it positioned me as a pioneer accompanied by some painful process.

The emphasis wasn't to build according to just any kind of pattern but 'the pattern'- that pattern prescribed by God for me.

I want you to pause momentarily and consider this; God has designed you for a particular purpose. Something uniquely planned for you to fulfil.

About Jesus, we read in **Hebrews 12:1-2- [New King James Version]:**

1 Therefore we also, since we are surrounded by so great a cloud of witnesses, let us lay aside every weight, and the sin which so easily ensnares us, and let us run with endurance the race that is set before us,

2 looking unto Jesus, the author and finisher of our faith, who for the joy that was set before Him endured the cross, despising the shame, and has sat down at the right hand of the throne of God.

Jesus' willingness and ability to endure the cross and despise the shame was predicated on the knowledge and revelation of the joy set before you.

I was pulled away from my own desire and towards God's divine will.

This pull was painful, costly and risky because of the nature of travelling to Ukraine for the gospel at that time, but I had to be there. It was a PULL. And the pull was not selective of our inclinations. On the contrary, it will draw you away from your inclinations.

Paul was given a thorn in his flesh. A messenger of Satan was on assignment to buffet him; he prayed three times but received grace to stay in the process, which was particularly his pull.

2 Corinthians 12:7 [King James Version]

"And lest I should be exalted above measure through the abundance of the revelations, there was given to me a thorn in the flesh, the messenger of Satan to buffet me, lest I should be exalted above measure."

Most times, God will not necessarily obliterate the enemy literally, but He would instead work on you to remove the effects of the enemy in your mind.

This means God's not working on the enemy, but He's working on you.

God knows that unless you are PULLED to him, you tend to give up on the first encounter with any opposition.

In many cases, the problem is not the enemy but our minds.

'Be transformed by renewing your mind' - Your thinking and thought-producing faculty control your life.

Exodus 13:17-18 [New International Version]

17 When Pharaoh let the people go, God did not lead them on the road through the Philistine country, though that was shorter. For God said, "If they face war, they might change their minds and return to Egypt."

18 So God led the people around by the desert road toward the Red Sea. The Israelites went up out of Egypt ready for battle.

If your mind cannot handle God's promises, they won't be released to you.

The pull from God creates the capacity in us to receive His release to us.

God has prepared a table for you, but you have to prepare for the table.

Being PULLED is not a negative to you; it is not a disadvantage, although it seems that way.

It takes people with spiritual insight and understanding, like the apostle Paul to appreciate adverse situations.

What is the Release?

The word release is associated with the following;

1. To be free

2. To be allowed to express

3. To be made available

Yes, we want to cast out demons, but we must first spend time with the father.

Yes, we want to take Nations, but we must first give ourselves to God, stay in His presence, drink from His well, soak in His presence, and build the relationship that brings revelation.

Jacob had to send his family away in Genesis 32:22 -, stayed alone, wrestled with God, had his hip touched, and had a name change.

In verse 30, he named the place Peniel, meaning the face of God, for he said I have seen God face to face, yet my life has been spared.

We have to be pulled into that place of being alone with God. When you get pulled, you leave everything and stay in God's presence.

The story of Joseph comes to mind, who, even though he had a PROMISE and was consciously aware of it, seems to be held back, remanded, halted, and restrained from going further.

The furtherance of his vision was expedited through restraint.

It appears that being sold, betrayed, falsely accused and forgotten fast-tracked the fulfilment of his dream.

31

So, what he initially saw as an attack from his brothers was a divine orchestration to advance his purpose.

Genesis 50:18-20 - [Amplified Bible]

18 Then his brothers went and fell down before him [in confession]; then they said, "Behold, we are your servants (slaves)." 19 But Joseph said to them, "Do not be afraid, for am I in the place of God? [Vengeance is His, not mine.] 20 As for you, you meant evil against me, but God meant it for good in order to bring about this present outcome, that many people would be kept alive [as they are this day].

The above scripture highlights that what you see as delay, denial or deprivation today may be the planning or coordination of the elements of that situation to produce a desired effect or result by God.

I call it a COVERT operation - an operation that is not openly acknowledged or displayed.

Reflecting on my early years of service in the ministry, it was almost all a covert operation. I had to embrace the discomforting and stretching processes to glean everything there was to get from it.

God did not state the reason for the service in detail while I was in the process. However, He required my complete dedication and commitment.

I pray that the shared personal experiences and scriptural examples outlined in this book will encourage and motivate you to yield to God's pull.

You may be hard pressed on every side, but you will not be crushed; perplexed, but not in despair;

You may be persecuted, but you will not be abandoned; struck down, but not destroyed.

You will always carry around in your body the death of Jesus so that the life of Jesus may also be revealed in your body.

We who are alive are always being given over to death for Jesus' sake so His life may also be revealed in our mortal bodies.

Please know that the sufferings of this present time are not worth being compared with the glory which shall be revealed in you.

-    2 Corinthians 4:8-12; Romans 8:18

PULLED ON PURPOSE

"Until the time that his word came: the word of the LORD tried him."

- **Psalm 105:19 [King James Version]**

Jesus lived 33 years, yet He changed the world through a ministry that lasted only three and a half years. Why throwing that at you right from the start?

The point is to help you draw reference from Jesus and realise that if your challenging days seem longer than your days of celebration, there may be purpose to that, and there are still opportunities to catch up and gain momentum for massive progress.

A position without preparation can become a disaster!

Given what you have not given yourself to can be detrimental to you. It can work against you. This is why preparation is necessary.

Moses was found by Pharaoh's daughter by divine orchestration, while every male Hebrew child was executed during his time.

He enjoyed the best boyhood as a prince of the most remarkable man on Earth in his days.

And it was likely a divine orchestration from God for Moses to be born in Egypt to gain valuable training and lessons because of the nature of his assignment and mandate.

Moses became one of the most significant people during the transition of the Israelites from Egypt to the land promised by God.

Moses' intense preparation, the twists and turns, the forfeiting of the pleasures of Pharoah's house, the saving of a Hebrew from the hand of an Egyptian, the rejection by the 2 fighting Hebrews, and his running away were all a set-up for what God had set up for him.

[Exodus 2:11-14]

It was all part of his preparation to lead. He had to understand the value system and know what is most important, he learnt how not to compromise or settle for temporary gratification, and he learnt problem-solving while becoming the leader God designed him to be.

24 By faith Moses, when he had grown up, refused to be known as the son of Pharaoh's daughter.

25 He chose to be mistreated along with the people of God rather than to enjoy the fleeting pleasures of sin.

26 He regarded disgrace for the sake of Christ as of greater value than the treasures of Egypt, because he was looking ahead to his reward.

27 By faith he left Egypt, not fearing the king's anger; he persevered because he saw him who is invisible.

Hebrews 11:24-27 [New International Version]

Joshua was 85 years old when he took over from Moses and died at 110, around 1406 B.C. Before assuming the commander-in-chief of the Host of Israel, Joshua had been a servant, a soldier and a spy.

God's principles requires preparation—the valley every legitimate heir of the blessing needs to thread before they rise and rule on the mountain of grace, glory and power.

Preparation has been proven to preserve promotion and positions of grace. Anyone who tries to ignore or escape preparation is on the waitlist for disaster! Esau was positioned as the firstborn ahead of Jacob, but soon he sold his birth right and eternal blessings for a hot meal on a hungry afternoon.

"We must all suffer from one of two pains: the pain of discipline or the pain of regret. The difference is discipline weighs ounces while regret weighs tons."

- ***Jim Rohn***

Do you hear the voices within telling you: This is not where your mates are; you should be far ahead by now; there's more out there for you; you're wasting time; your pain is meaningless?

Do these questions make you feel stuck, alone and ashamed? Does life feel like moving in circles while others are making massive progress?

Even though you think you deserve more, are you struggling with less?

If you answer yes to any of these questions, this book has some answers!

What if I tell you that you're in the process of the most significant breakthrough you've ever seen?

39

I don't know if you believe where you are is not too far from the manifestation of God's glory in your life.

Can your eyes shift off your struggles and anxiety to what God is working out in your life for one moment?

You see, the enemy enjoys how you're letting that situation get complicated, thereby delaying your miracles because you're cooperating with him—unaware of what God is doing in and through you.

Many are drawn to the possibility of tremendous results. They want to progress with minimal preparation.

"Before everything else, getting ready is the secret of success."

In 1929 Henry Ford, an American industrialist, the founder of the Ford Motor Company, and sponsor of the development of the assembly line technique of mass production, was asked if there is a secret to success, and he responded, *"Certainly. I know two people who have found*

it.

He went further to respond, "Getting ready. Getting

prepared. There were Edison and Lindbergh—they both got

ready before they started. I had to find that out, too. I had

to stop 10 years after I had started—I had to stop for 10

years and get ready. I made my first car in 1893, but it was

1903 before I had it ready to sell. It is these simple things

that young men ought to know, and they are the hardest to

grasp. Before everything else, get ready. When I say

"before everything else," I know it includes almost

everything else."

But we must understand that getting ready has a different timeframe for everyone.

Henry Ford had to stop for 10 years and get ready.

The discipline and sacrifice of what I call a 'start-stop-start' cannot be overemphasised.

41

There is no shame in stopping if you have to and starting again because of the benefits of preparation. Get ready.

The results of an unprepared life are predictable. Things we never expected would happen *do* happen—and they occur quicker than the things we hoped would happen. The reason is simple: hoping for something without preparing for it places us at a disadvantage, while preparation puts us at an advantage even when what we hoped for is delayed.

Unpreparedness can disconnect you from a potentially beneficial opportunity. Therefore, we must learn to enjoy the season of preparation because our present troubles (worry, concerns) are minor and will only last for a while. Yet they produce for us a glory that vastly outweighs them... (2 Corinthians 4:17).

Today, we want to get invited everywhere to speak, thousands waiting to get a glimpse of our glory and the avalanche of our wisdom. We wish to be the one that determines who listens to us, where we travel and the magnitude of our audience. But my friend, these things are not fixed by us. God determines our results and the audience based on the wisdom of His will and our ability to walk in step with the purpose and preparation He has structured for our destiny. From the size and quality of our audience to the kind of results we crave, God's hand is responsible for our destiny.

You cannot IMAGINE how big-of-a-purpose God is preparing you for

But, as it is written, "What no eye has seen, nor ear heard, nor the heart of man imagined, what God has prepared for those who love him."

1 Corinthians 2:9

God's ways are far above and beyond what we can imagine. In the scripture above, Apostle Paul lets you and I realise the future for us. God is beyond our budget for life and boundaries for success. He sets systems in place to prepare us for platforms and possibilities we can hardly imagine for ourselves. Here's one reason why I believe God is in charge of our destinies beyond what our minds can conceive:

While growing up in the faith, my focus was primarily on serving God within the confines of a local church with no intention of being actively involved in any form of ministry leadership. And when I grew to become part of ministry leadership, my idea was to be a local residential pastor, not seeing beyond the scope of the four walls. I didn't know anything about being called to the marketplace. Therefore, the consideration of combining ministry and marketplace was something wrong. I never understood anything about mentoring, coaching, teaching, or setting up all these businesses I'm presently involved in. Yet, God knew the potential in me, the preparations I have been through, and the platforms where I would manifest what He has embedded in me beyond my wildest dreams. Another point to underscore here is that, as I reflected, I never knew the requirements and ramifications of that process consciously.

My understanding was to do what was required of me at that time, no matter how challenging they presented themselves. Perhaps I was training undercover and unaware of it.

From my experience, we must be trained undercover and unaware in various areas of ministry and life when necessary, allowing us to focus on that area without distraction.

The story of David illustrates how looking after his father's sheep and goat, fighting for them and protecting them from the lion and bear would translate into leading an entire nation unknown to him as there was no prior conversation or directive that was a training ground.

The knowledge, skill, confidence, and victory David garnered from defeating the lion and bear became a valuable reference point and motivation when the challenge of Goliath presented itself as an opportunity in disguise. (1 Samuel 17:34-37)

God often positions us for training in a particular area of life without realising the bigger picture of why we are there.

A wealthy individual who owns an automobile business may deploy his son, the heir to his wealth, to work in the janitorial department of the company. Before bringing him close to the management team, he may move the kid from janitorial to electrical, mechanic, technology, and sales. And this wealthy owner may only do all this without clearly informing his son of the purpose of the move around.

He expects the son to focus on any particular area of the business he is deployed to, accept that position, focus on the job and consider it his place of operation.

The son, therefore, is placed under various managers to learn the importance of collaborative working, how to be under authority and taking directives from people. He also will learn the operations of the business from the ground level.

The purpose of this exercise set by the father is to bring his son to a place of maturity because that would bring sustainability and longevity and guarantee generational wealth. Rather than just handing him the business, he intends to build something in his son, instil some valuable life lessons and establish a system of operation in him. Lessons that may be difficult to learn by mere conversation.

He didn't want to give the business to his son. The father wants to put the business in the son.

I learnt this growing up;

What you put inside your children will outlast what you put in their hands. Your investment in their development is more valuable than the disbursement you give them.

This illustration is seen in the bible when it says;

"Now what I mean when I talk about children and their guardians is this: as long as the heir is a child, he does not differ at all from a slave even though he is the future owner and master of all the estate;

² but he is under the authority of guardians and household administrators or managers until the date set by his father, when he is of legal age."

- Galatians 4:1-2 (The Amplified Bible)

How intriguing is this? Though he is the future owner and master of all the estate, he can't access it and fully operate in it until a set age, time, or an expected behavioural level.

We must understand that training is necessary for what we will occupy and operate in. These training pieces form the father's expectation regarding our occupancy or possession of what He has promised. But we are not given a detailed explanation.

The Bible gives some insight into this dilemma in 1 Corinthians 2:9, The Amplified Bible; *"But just as it is written in Scripture, Things which the eye has not seen and the ear has not heard, and which have not entered the heart of man, all that God has prepared for those who love Him, who hold Him in affectionate reverence, who obey Him, and who gratefully recognize the benefits that He has bestowed"*

Let's look at it from the microscope of a football coach and his players. Usually, due to experience and exposure, a skilled coach can study an ongoing game and carefully implement a particular drill or strategy practised on the training ground since they watch the play of events from the side-line. The coach would run several formations and playing patterns during practice to prepare the players for these instances since they never fully understood what the opposition would present them on game day. And for this to be effective, the players must learn to comply with varying playing formations and drills.

Look at where you were yesterday.

When you understand where you are in the process of divine preparation, you will walk in realms of possibilities without being tied down by prevailing circumstances. There's a chokehold of ignorance that I've seen in many people who refuse to pay attention to the possibilities God has revealed to them.

I had learnt to see beyond my limitations every time, even when all I had was a big heart and a massive vision— which involved amplifying the place God had destined me to be while diminishing my present limitations. I was visualising everything I was saying.

The visualisation allows me to see beyond all the rubbish and posture me to see every piece of resource required for my assignment. I knew that it is coming to a time when it didn't matter where I lived, it didn't matter how small I looked on the outside, yet the world 'won't be able to resist my sound—queens, kings, and people in leadership positions will come to the brightness of my shinning. But you must understand that my confession was not predicated on my present situation.; because I 'didn't look like what I was confessing. Instead, my confession was fuelled by what I could see through the lenses of faith, the associated processes, and the preparation I was exposed to.

It became clear that some of the circumstances we are experiencing can become indicators pointing us in the direction of what has been destined for us. Therefore, instead of considering your adverse circumstances as deterrents, let them become motivating factors that'll propel you to achieve the greatness God has destined for you.

Can you speak possibilities into your life right now? Remember, shift your focus from the current pain and problem and channel that investment into the glorious realities God has revealed to you. But you have to speak from a place of revelation. It can be delusional to attempt to release what has not been released to you by God. Speaking from information is one level, but revelation gives you the real power that empowers you to persevere in facing obstacles. Revelation will often foster resilience.

You must keep your eyes on Jesus and understand that the pull is for your release!

CONSIDER DAVID - A KING IN A KID.

Every person who considers fulfilling the purpose of God must go through a season of intense preparation. For David, his preparation time was in obscurity, where he served as a shepherd over his father's sheep. His encounter and victory over the different wild animals constituted his training ground, the process and platform God used to set him up for the future He had prepared for him. It is essential to highlight that God may not necessarily send unfavourable situations our way, but He can use them to our advantage. But we must be sensitive to the things happening around us.

A demonstration of this point was Joseph and his brothers. 'Joseph's response to his brothers in Genesis 50:19-21, the Common English Bible was:

[19] But Joseph said to them, "Don't be afraid. Am I God? [20] You planned something bad for me, but God

produced something good from it, in order to save the lives of many people, just as he's doing today. [21] Now, don't be afraid. I will take care of you and your children." So he put them at ease and spoke reassuringly to them.

How often have we abandoned the preparation process because it seems contrary to what we initially expected? How often have we left lessons and tests designed to bring the best out of us, pull the melodies out of us, and pull greatness out of us?

In Genesis 22, we were introduced to how God tested Abraham.

Genesis 22:1-5

After these things, God tested Abraham and said to him, "Abraham"! And he said, "Here I am".

2 He said, "Take your son, your only son Isaac, whom you love, and go to the land of Moriah, and offer him there as a burnt offering on one of the mountains of which I shall tell you".

3 So Abraham rose early in the morning, saddled his donkey, and took two of his young men with him and his son Isaac. And he cut the wood for the burnt offering and arose and went to the place of which God had told him.

4 On the third day, Abraham lifted up his eyes and saw the place from afar.

5 Then Abraham said to his young men, "Stay here with the donkey; I and the boy will go over there and worship and come again to you".

A few points that interested me from this account of Abraham are:

1. There was no indication that God informed him that this instruction was a test, illustrating that God doesn't have to notify us before the time of preparation, nor will He inform us about our seasons of tests and trials.

2. Abraham's response was swift. His speedy response suggests that he wasn't hesitant to respond to God's instructions. He left very early in the morning.

Where are you on the path of preparation? Are you settled or set up for a pull? Why don't you give that vision, idea, and ministry a reckless abandon, a pull for a release, and the necessary preparation because, in due time, you'll reap if you faint not?

Your career, business, ministry, or anything you are involved with can take a new turn if you apply the right approach— preparation for the greater you.

David was anointed as king when he was a youth. He only became king once he got released. He was pulled, and he got released.

Sometimes, a release initiates another pull. So, it becomes like a cycle; a release will trigger a pull. A new level of growth introduces you to a different set of training. Every new level of achievement requires from you a different kind of commitment and sacrifice.

For every process that leads you to a place, that place then becomes a new process. So, with Joseph's experience, his brothers sold him. It was a process. He started another life with the people who bought him; he got into trouble and was imprisoned because of an accusation from Potiphar's wife.

Although the prison eliminated the problem he faced from Potiphar's wife, it began a new process for him that fast-tracked him to the palace.

Joseph's arrival at the palace was a settled place for him and potentially could end his processes. But when Pharaoh died, and another Pharoah who did not have a relationship with Joseph replaced him, it became a new process for him again.

So, the release often becomes an introduction to the new pull. Abraham's life exemplified that as well. Suppose we consider our walk with God like a string; the depth of our pull can determine the extent of our release.

It can be painful when you are pulled into Him. But the loud sound it produces is heard when the strings are pulled and released. So, let's be patient.

IT ALL BEGINS WITH A PULL

"Like arrows are in the hand of a warrior, so are children of one's youth. Happy is the man who has his quiver full of them; They shall not be ashamed but shall speak with their enemies in the gate."

-Psalm 127:4-5 (NKJV)

An empty quiver spells shame and trouble in battle. Every warrior knows just the criticality of arrows and what he must do before his arrows are battle-ready. So, battle arrows are pulled back for the momentum required to hit their preset aim.

The scripture above can be translated as children are blessing from God and arrows to defeat the enemy. Doubtless, God has a purpose for every child. However, I want you to know that God is not just interested in our childhood. He's committed to our entire life stages and

59

future realities. Every man and woman are an arrow in the hand of God—in God's quiver. But let's first consider how the arrow was produced.

How did mere wood in the bush become an arrow in the warrior's quiver?

I bet you know that arrows journey from sticks picked up and sharpened to become pointed enough to hit a target with maximum impact and precision. But imagine the stick, pulled off from the rest of the piles in the woods, wondering why it was chosen from the crowd into a life for a selected few. Sometimes the stick wishes that seclusion is all there is to worry about, but no. There comes filing and sharpening—the pain of preparation. Even then, the arrow feels ready, but there's more that it must bear. It must wait in the quiver until it's its turn and in the bow during the targeting. Unaware of when the time to launch out, the arrow endures being pulled back as the warrior strains the strings and stretches it for a perfect aim.

I can imagine the arrow wondering why the delay. I thought I was ready. You can almost hear the string straining to keep itself together as the warrior pulls it backwards at length.

Like the arrows and the string, we start with God, not knowing everything about what we're designed and potentiated to achieve. I was kept from completely understanding what was required to accomplish my future promises. However, God, by His divine orchestration, by the infinite decisive master plan, has structured me, has curated all these activities that I've been through in my childhood till today to ensure that all the exposure, the failures, the down moments, the up moments, the lessons, the friendships, all the alignments, the collaborations, everything that I've been through have put everything together to ensure I was ready for this moment. As I write, I've only seen a glimpse of glory. I still do not know the fullness of The Almighty.

With God, there is no wasteful experience. Like a master builder, God engages everything we have experienced in life as resources for our development and displays His excellent work.

I still live like Paul, wanting "to grab hold of why he grabbed hold of me." (Philippians 3:12).

I want to comprehend glory, goodness, and miracles, but I believe there's more! Why did you pick me? Why was I arrested and detained in the circumference of your plan? I think you're also asking God—no matter where you are in fulfilling God's purpose for your life— why did you pull me to yourself?

Why did God pull you?

In life, we go through a series of situations that throw questions at us, like the sea currents. We navigate storms that wreck our ship until all we have is just a lifejacket and many unanswered questions. Does this pain have a purpose? Is God aware of where I am? Has God forgotten His promises towards me? Is there a light at the end of this darkness? How did I crash into this valley?

In the middle of life's storms, we have two choices: Throwing in the towel, curling up, and giving up or turning to God for comfort and strength till the storm is over. Walking with God from the valley of the shadows of fear and questions requires the power of knowing who God is and what He is preparing at the end of the storm.

Apostle Paul said 'that I may know Him and the power of his resurrection and the fellowship of His suffering, being conformable to His death.

I press towards the mark of the high calling.

I want to know, why did you pull me? This is a crucial cry!

Why did you pull me to yourself? What is the reason? What kind of sound do you want me to produce? What kind of sound do you want the world to hear from me?

The pull relates to our uniqueness.

Have you ever wondered why we are all drawn to different genres of music? Have you ever wondered why certain sounds get your attention?

Have you thought of why a particular sound produces a different reaction from you when heard?

Certain people wouldn't align with your work or vision, no matter how good it appears and how pure your intentions are. This response is because, just like the sound of a musical tune, we all tend to gravitate toward certain kinds of music, a sound that appeals to us.

I lead an organisation with several community initiatives, but not everyone will find all the projects interesting. People will give their support to the project that resonates with them. The one they can connect with.

We, therefore, must learn not to take it personally when people don't respond positively to a particular vision or idea we put before them. The idea doesn't make a melodic sound in their minds and hearts. But one day, another time, or another project may excite them and make them fully commit to your actions. That is when you know you've pulled a cord and released a sound.

As the sound of your voice, when your time has come to walk into your prophetic inheritance, you will release a sound that resonates with people. For the first time, your voice will pull the heartstrings of many because you have been pulled to release the sound that changes people forever!

Now notice that the day of your manifestation is not the first day you are speaking to people, trying to get them to respond.

They have been hearing or listening to you before, seeing what you do, but they never really heard you.

Your Word is Coming.

"Until the time that his word came: the word of the LORD tried him."

-Psalm 105:19 (KJV Bible)

You have been singing, but they have not heard the note that stirs their soul. Now, they are hearing that note. Why? Because your time has come. It moves people because now you have been pulled in a different direction for releasing that sound of influence.

God doesn't pull us only in one way, you know. You have been drawn to different places under different circumstances. However, a sound has come out of you; you've been released! The stretch and strain paid off! You've been released to produce a particular sound, setting people free.

When people most times say, oh! Your season has come; they mean it's time for your release. Just be grateful that

66

your moment of pull has yielded off. And so, with an energised response and the working and power of the Holy Spirit, move into manifestation! In Jesus Name!

Dive into the next chapter and let me show you how Abraham was pulled for his memorable generational impact.

THE PULL IS DYNAMIC

God's chronological blessings are consistent with trials and testing. Without any gainsaying, tough times could be a blessing in God's hand. It could be the seasons where the flowers fail to bloom, and the fig tree does not blossom. All these do not mean it is against you or your progress. As children of God, we ought to be sure about His eternal plan for us. His plan may allow some difficulties into our lives that may seem to ruin all the goals and ambitions we have for ourselves, which may ultimately result in good in the long run if handled correctly.

The primary goal of God's perfect plan is to reveal His glory to humanity. He does this by allowing us to share in His cup and His suffering.

Suffering is not something anyone wants to identify with. However, having a revelation of the purpose for the suffering can be instrumental in strengthening our faith in God and growing our relationship with Him. It is with this understanding that the Apostle Paul writes;

"The very credentials these people are waving around as something special, I'm tearing up and throwing out with the trash—along with everything else I used to take credit for. And why? Because of Christ. Yes, all the things I once thought were so important are gone from my life. Compared to the high privilege of knowing Christ Jesus as my Master, firsthand, everything I once thought I had going for me is insignificant—dog dung. I've dumped it all in the trash so that I could embrace Christ and be embraced by him. I didn't want some petty, inferior brand of righteousness that comes from keeping a list of rules when I could get the robust kind that comes from trusting Christ—God's righteousness.

10-11 *I gave up all that inferior stuff so I could know Christ personally, experience his resurrection power, be a partner in his suffering, and go all the way with him to death itself.*

If there was any way to get in on the resurrection from the dead, I wanted to do it."

- Philippians 3:7-9 [The Message Translation]

I am always intrigued by Paul's thought pattern and his approach towards embracing and teaching the gospel, including painful moments. No wonder he is recorded as one of the greatest Apostles who ever lived and wrote most of the New Testament.

He draws parallels in his exposure to painful encounters and knowing God intimately. But the question then is, did he get to have better knowledge of God because of the challenges he faced? Or did he possess the faith and ability to convert his exposure to painful encounters into meaningful milestones?

It suffices to say that Paul's emphasis on suffering, pain or willingness to experience the death and resurrection of Christ was not the only way to knowing Christ and growing in faith. Instead, he intended to bring our attention to the possibility of using encounters considered as negatives to our advantage in building faith and a stronger relationship with God.

This is why irrespective of the challenges you might be experiencing right now, one thing is sure, God is working to ensure your beauty and glory are revealed to the world. He reiterates this in **Romans 8:28**, "*and we know that God causes all things to work together for good to those who love God, to those who are called according to His purpose.*"

John piper said something profound, "*God is glorified in us when satisfied with Him.*" This means that God's glory and beauty in our lives are connected to how much we give ourselves to Him - the more we yield our lives to God, the more the world sees significant changes in us, and the more we yield a bumper harvest of God's blessing.

Revelation of God's glory in us is predicated on our relationship with Him.

Exposure to glory is based on encounters with God.

Nevertheless, when we experience a sudden pull, situations that eat us up and stir up the world we are used to, we tend to become discouraged and start doubting God's goodness and love towards us.

As believers, the goodness of God is the fragrance of our souls. It entails the promises of God to us through the scriptures. Are you at any point in denial of the blessings of God due to the adverse situations you encounter? You may think the pull you are experiencing is overwhelming. However, you are expected to live to fullness in the light of God's promised blessings above the 'blessings' the world seems to hold for you.

In this chapter, we will examine God's promised blessings in Abraham's life. Not only this, but we will also study the various pulls he had and how he could withhold himself from the pleasures and distractions of life while awaiting the glory ahead.

The Father of Faith

Abraham, the father of faith, did not earn the title overnight. He was pulled in diverse unpleasant ways. His lifetime was punctuated with various tests and trials that would have made many mortal men fall in despair, but he still held on. How else would you explain the shameful delays, shocking requests, and staggering sacrifices God demanded from him? So indeed, his title as a father of faith is not a conferred honorary title. It was tested and tried in diverse ways and through challenging situations.

It is always easier for us to claim the blessings of Abraham and hold on to the promise of *heirdom* through the lineage of Abraham, but many times we hate the thought of going through

73

the same trials and tests that Abraham went through. So, the question is, how do we partake of the blessing if we avoid the testing?

How do we know how to maintain the glory when we only want to hear the story without having to experience the testing?

The truth is that God's love for us compels Him to prune us. To keep us in shape so we can be vessels unto honour. Vessels fit for the king's use. Stretching is one of the ways to grow; it is a factor for expansion and development.

There is a misconception that stretching is performed only by people in active sports. But stretching is recommended for all of us to protect our mobility and independence.

Some benefits of stretching are that it keeps the muscles flexible, strong, and healthy and that flexibility is needed to maintain a range of motion in the joints.

The danger of not stretching is that when we suddenly place a demand on the muscle for any activity, they need to be stronger and able to extend themselves as demanded. Because without stretching, our muscles shorten and become tight. This puts us at risk for joint pains, strains, and even muscle damage.

Against this backdrop, Paul's writing in Philippians 3:12-15 made it clear that he constantly reaches for more. He's never content with staying at one level. That sounds like stretching to me.

We, like Paul, must stretch, press, and desire more, even though that brings some discomfort, which is expected anyway.

12-14 I'm not saying that I have this all together, that I have it made. But I am well on my way, reaching out for Christ, who has so wondrously reached out for me. Friends, don't get me wrong: By no means do I count myself an expert in all of this, but I've got my eye on the goal, where God is beckoning us onward—to Jesus. I'm off and running, and I'm not turning back.

- **Philippians 3:12-14 [The** *Message Translation]*

Our position as sons within the kingdom of God is legitimised by discipline.

Contrary to the expectations of our flesh, discipline and correction are profitable because they are tools that qualify us to partake of God's holiness.

This thought of discipline is highlighted in the Message Translation of Hebrews 12:4-11:

4-11 In this all-out match against sin, others have suffered far worse than you, to say nothing of what Jesus went through—all that bloodshed! So don't feel sorry for yourselves. Or have you forgotten how good parents treat children and that God regards

you as his children?

My dear child, don't shrug off God's discipline,

  but don't be crushed by it either.

It's the child he loves that he disciplines;

  the child he embraces, he also corrects.

God is educating you; that's why you must never drop out. He's

treating you as dear children. This trouble you're in isn't

punishment; it's training, the normal experience of children. Only

irresponsible parents leave children to fend for themselves.

Would you prefer an irresponsible God? We respect our parents

for training and not spoiling us, so why not embrace God's

training so we can truly live? While we were children, our parents

did what seemed best to them. But God is doing what is best for

us, training us to live God's holy best. At the time, discipline isn't

much fun. It always feels like it's going against the grain. Later,

of course, it pays off big-time, for it's the well-trained who find

themselves mature in their relationship with God.

'It is the well-trained who find themselves mature in their relationship with God.'

A basketball player needs to stretch to find any form of release in his game.

God stretches us. He pulls us to release the hidden potentials locked inside of us. This pull may come to us and manifest in different forms and patterns that vary from individual to individual.

It means that your pull might be different from your friend's. For example, your pull may come in finances because of the weight of the assignment for kingdom finance upon you. Your friend's pull may be in delayed childbirth because there is a lesson in their experience connected to the virtue of patience and faith, just like Abraham. However, whichever area we might be experiencing difficulty in the area of pull, our confidence should be bolstered by God's eternal and mighty love for our lives.

It is essential to underline that God's discipline is always motivated by love.

The Pull of God

Wait! This feat does not promise to be an easy one. It may not be a smooth ride through the tides of trials. The road may be too dark for you while you stumble through the darkness in disappointment, difficulty, disaster and despair. An isolated place where your family, friends and companions have turned their backs against you, just like in the case of Job. Do you feel the pull stretching you beyond your elastic limit, and you may snap at any moment, losing it all to the burden too much to bear?

You may be searching for answers trying to **see this "bad situation" as a "good situation in disguise."** However, always remember that these pulls are God's way of disciplining His children to grow as they mature spiritually.

Have you ever considered why raw gold passes through the fire before it can be refined and pure?

Why does a guitarist need to pull their cord while playing it?

Before a transformation can occur, there must be a test we are unaware of its duration.

No wonder the scriptures say, "*a day to the Lord is like a thousand years, and a thousand years is as one day." [2 Peter 3:8]*. How do you get to calculate that?

The music, the imminent sound, determines how the string is pulled and for how long. When the Lord pulls you like a guitarist hits the guitar, you can see the apparent short distance, but the stretched string has no idea how long that pull would be. Because the way and timeframe the string is pulled depend on the music's rhythm.

Every pull produces a different sound.

In the same way, when God pulls us, it may be short in His eyes and the eyes of those around us, but for you going through the stretch, it may be an overly stressful and extended time.

Please understand that whatever your case might be, you need not worry. This pull might be a test of your faith and obedience to God. At a time like this, you might find your perspectives changing, and your faith diminishes due to people's derogatory comments. Yet, you must stand firm and embrace God, the trustworthy source of all blessings. Why? He is working to lead you through the end of the tunnel, where the light shines over the darkness of your life. Apostle Paul rightly opines, *"For our light and momentary affliction is preparing us for an eternal weight of glory beyond all comparison"* (**2 Corinthians 4:17**). To help us grow, here are practical ways to scale the hurdles of the pull effect.

Activate your Faith.

The activation of our faith often comes through our trials; for instance, Abraham became a father of faith through the work of faith.

When faced with the challenge of leaving his father's land for an unknown country, he didn't waste time by querying God. He would have asked, "How can I? What are you saying, God? Leave my father, my mum? Come on, God! Where do you want me to go? This is family, you know? What are you saying?" This is my family; I love them. Instead, he exercised a high degree of faith in God and took his wife and all he owned to a land he didn't know.

Perhaps you think leaving one's family is not a big deal; imagine someone telling you to excuse yourself from your relations and ask you to go on a journey to a strange land; what would your reaction be? It could lead to resistance. But like Abraham, you need to activate your faith to change the trajectory of your life.

In between the pull and the release lies the cord that looks small but powerful. The cord is your faith. You must trust in the Lord consistently with your consciousness and mindset. Do not allow anything to cut the cord of your life. It is a gateway to the supernatural.

Abraham was tested again when God told him to separate from Lot, his nephew. Some can relate to what Abraham passed through with the sentiment of giving a son or daughter in marriage, particularly with the possibility of them relocating to a different and far country. It breaks your heart. Yet Abraham activated his faith, obeyed, and reaped the lasting benefit.

The Inevitable Friend

How do you walk with the Lord when you are being pulled without clarity of vision? How do you know which way to go without help? You need a guide. The Holy Spirit is looking for people to show God's mysteries. People willing to wait, stay and dwell in the secret place- A place far from your comfort zone. It may not be visible to others or a sight too attractive to behold, yet it has the power to transform our entire lives and generation. It can shape us through that place of preparation, that place of transformation, that place of refining, and that place of testing, to the land that God has ordained for us.

According to John Nelson Darby," *the presence of the Holy Spirit is the keystone of all our hopes"* when we are down and in despair, it is the Holy Spirit that strengthens us, giving us the hope and the comfort to keep trusting in the unfailing promises of God for us.

Live in Obedience

The willingness to follow through with every instruction of God is the key that opens up the gates of God's blessing. Again, Abraham was pulled when God said, *"go and sacrifice your boy"*. God wanted to pull him differently to ascertain how much he was willing to go with him and if he would produce a different sound.

We are bound to experience one or a series of tests, especially as believers. After we think this one is over, then it's another. But can God trust us to the extent of placing us in various situations to produce different tunes, just as a guitarist would pull his strings differently for other themes?

Just as Job said," *"But He knows the way I take; When He has put me to the test, I will come out as gold* (Job 23:10).

When we look closely at the confession from Job in the bible verse above, what captures my interest is the word 'tests'.

Surprisingly that's the word we most likely disconnect from because of the experiences associated with it. However, the failure to grasp and completely embrace that word is part of the reason many of us have yet to obtain the promise. God has already given the promise, but it can be obtained after pruning, purging, or tests.

Galatians 4:1-2, the J.B. Phillips New Testament translation sheds some light on this:

But you must realise that so long as an heir is a child, though he is destined to be master of everything, he is, in practice, no different from a servant. He has to obey a guardian or trustee until the time which his father has chosen for him to receive his inheritance.

Access to what the heir is destined for is linked to maturity.

Maturity is synonymous with sensibleness, development, and experience. But there can be no experience without an encounter.

You cannot have a crown without combat. And you cannot call yourself a conqueror without a battle.

When we face similar challenging situations like Job, we must be confident that GOD knows our destination. The different pulls we face are part of the developmental growth we need to experience.

Having this perspective will change our approach to many of the things we are dealing with and the ones we will encounter in the future. It will help us live a life of obedience and trust.

Just like Jesus. God didn't fully reveal the extent of His suffering to him. Who would have thought Christ would also be pulled the way He was during His earthly ministry? Jesus served his ministry here on earth by doing the will of God. The people He loved most and did great things for turned their backs and persecuted him. They were the same ones who spat at him, pierced his side, and scourged the crown of thorns on his skull.

Yet, when Jesus said, *"thy will be done"*, God did not tell him the nature of suffering He was going to experience. Even with the prophecies spoken ages ago. What was written by Prophet Isaiah was that *"he was bruised for our transgressions, he was chastised, and the punishment that brought us peace was upon him, and by His stripes, we are healed"*, but there was no definite description of what his pain might be. Sometimes God leads us in unfamiliar ways without fully revealing the whole extent we may go. But what He needs from us is obedience: total surrender, yield and pliability to His will.

LEARN TO RELEASE AND LET GO

Sometimes God will make harsh demands on us; just as he asked Abraham to release and sacrifice Isaac, he may be requesting you right now. For instance, God has told people to leave specific religious organisations and places where they were welcomed and were flourishing to an unfamiliar place where they knew no one.

I have been in that situation before when I left my first church in Nigeria, where I grew as a new believer to join another. I was already on the verge of becoming a church plant leader at my first church. At that point in my life, the instruction came from God to leave where I was fellowshipping to a new church where I didn't know anybody.

I moved from being a well-respected minister to sitting as part of the congregation –lost in the crowd.

That was challenging for me, as I was already in a place of prominence where people knew me. I served in different capacities. I led prayer in this big church, conducted deliverances at people's houses, and was a leader in the prayer ministry. I was also part of the senior pastor's protocol and travelled with him; I was close to my leadership. So people knew me very well. Imagine being asked to leave all that and pulled to a place where I was a stranger and unknown. Come on! You got to be serious, God; what is this about? I obeyed, followed necessary protocols and moved. But this didn't seem fair at all.

We miss it because many seek fairness and popularity instead of obeying God.

I've learned to obey God against popular opinion. Even my pastor, at the time, laughed; he did not fully understand. But I understood his plight: he loved me like a son. You don't want to let someone go quickly if you love them to that extent. That is the truth. My love for my pastor is still intact today. We still talk and are in touch with each other. I love and adore him from the bottom of my heart, and I don't blame him for what happened. Perhaps I would have done the same thing he did in his shoes.

If anyone who has stayed so close to me and has been with me the way I was with my pastor came and said they were leaving for another place, even if I want to release you, I would be pained. So, it is quite natural for him to resist letting me go, but eventually, he called the missions pastor, saying, *"go and pray for him and let him go"*.

After that, I went, joined a church as a newbie, and sat in the congregation. It was a different experience compared to the church where I was coming from. It was like being pulled down from a high rank. But I didn't let that deter me. I knew God had more excellent things planned for me, even though I didn't completely understand it. I gave myself entirely to the service of God in obedience. I allowed myself to be pulled, and God moved me where He wanted me to be and is still moving me. He placed me on strategic tables I had no business sitting at

91

because of sheer obedience. He gave me access to people, places, and things I never could imagine. This is why we must be willing to be pulled and lifted. I grew in ranks and was released, my sound was heard, and that sound is blessing people.

None of us chooses the audience that God has destined for us. God determines the audience.

I know that because while growing up in ministry, my idea about ministry was to serve my pastor. I didn't know anything about being called to the marketplace. I never understood anything about mentoring, coaching, business teaching, or setting up all these business things I'm setting up.

I knew nothing about it. No one deliberately taught me anything about it. Still, God, by his divine orchestration, by the divine infinite decisive master plan has structured me, has curated all these activities that I've been through in my childhood till today to ensure that all the exposure, the failures, the down moments, the up moments, the lessons, the friendships, all the alignments, the collaborations, everything that I've been through have put everything together to ensure it is set for this moment. Even yet, I still do not know the fullness of Him who called me, who pulled me according to His divine will.

I still press…that is why Paul said…I want to grab hold of why He grabbed hold of me. I want to comprehend why I was apprehended. I like that one. Why did you arrest me? Why did you pull me to yourself?

That I may know him and the power of his resurrection and the fellowship of his suffering, being conformable to his death. I press towards the mark of the high calling. I want to know, "why did you pull me?" This is a cry. "Why did you pull me to yourself?" What is the reason? What kind of sound do you want me to produce? What kind of sound do you want the world to hear from me?

Have an Open Heart

Paula Rinehart said, *"In the place of gracious uncertainty, we wait for the broken places to be brought back together. For the meaning of our suffering to be revealed in His. For the righteous reign of a mighty God, whose goodness we will spend all eternity celebrating. We wait – with open, expectant hearts."*

God has called us to a life of abundance where he intends for us to live our best lives. He presents opportunities in the form of trials and opens doors in the form of challenges. The best way to grasp what God is doing in our lives is to open our hands and hearts to his pruning and discipline. Having an open heart is a sign that we accept the Lordship of Christ over the situations we are faced with.

Abraham had no clue where he was going, but he trusted God and counted it as righteousness. Likewise, God keeps records of our hearts and attitudes toward His instructions and leading. When He pulls us to know if the sound we produce is whining and complaining, he pulls us to understand our deepest thoughts. But when we serve him with an open heart and a clear conscience, our tune becomes melodious to all who hear us.

The Key to Intimacy and Dependency

One thing I am sure of, God is not in the business of speaking to people who are not interested in building intimacy by depending on Him. That's true! God has no intention to test us beyond our capacity. This is why He places us in a position to prepare our conception so that the execution would be easy. Therefore, we should learn to trust and rely on Him no matter how hard it may seem.

God tested Abraham's dependency on him during his separation from his nephew, Lot.

When the time came for Lot to leave, God instructed Abraham to allow Lot first to choose his portion of land. That is a different kind of pull. We find ourselves in a similar situation when engaging in a personal or business relationship, and God instructs us to separate from them without deciding on the outcome.

God may prompt us to allow them to have the privilege of making what would appear to be the deciding move before us.

Allowing them to make the first move or pick may seem unfair. But it is essential to know that fairness may not be an issue regarding God's dealing with us. It's about trust, dependence, about reliance. When we look at our lives, how often do we miss God's pull because we're trying to be fair and independent? How often do we miss God's lesson on discipline because we try to be socially or politically correct? We want to stand out as a firm business mind in our time; hence we make decisions contrary to God's instructions. Sometimes we must learn to allow others to go first, pick first, and speak first.

As simple as this may sound, it may be the most humbling experience for some.

Be Resilient

Part of the lesson from fitness is that resistance produces results. Sometimes the trials God throws at us are not to crush us but to build our spiritual muscles. It creates a platform where resistance produces results.

During one of my travels, I checked into a hotel whose fitness suite had basic pieces of equipment and I quickly discovered how easily one can miss out on the opportunity to exercise because of how basic the equipment is and the result you could produce with it.

Though the equipment in the fitness suite is simple, when I walked in, my question was, how do I create the maximum resistance to get optimum results? How do I engage basic to get the best achievement?

How do I make the most of what I've been given?

Do I complain about the card I have been dealt, or do I creatively become productive with it?

Do I complain about the type of equipment in that hotel fitness suite, or do I become innovative?

No matter how simple you are or how the people you are around, don't take what seems easy for granted; pay attention to the simplicity of any provision and don't take it for granted.

Easy things can produce tremendous benefits. Because something is easy does not mean it cannot be gratifying.

I have learnt not to take the simplicity of any situation for granted. Through my experience in fitness, I have learnt how to intentionally create an increased amount of resistance, even in a basic environment, to produce an optimal beneficial result. This is described as putting pressure on yourself to produce the desired outcome. It is engaging what seems easy and delivering an exceptional impact.

For many, we have walked out on strategic opportunities because they needed to appear more satisfactory; they looked easy; therefore, we undermined and undervalued the provision and sometimes our assignment.

But something look easy does not mean it is not of value.

My prayer for you reading this now is to have a revelation - for God to open your eyes to see beyond the physical because a revelation will bring you appreciation.

The day God opens your eyes to what you have been assigned, you will begin to handle it differently, regardless of who supports you and whether it is less appealing.

Research shows that those who like what they do and have become very successful doing it are those who found something easy and worked hard at it.

These people also know that because a thing is easy to do, it is also easy not to do it. This is why many people are still where they are. What they have or can do looks easy but can bring them financial freedom if they choose to work hard at it.

Knowing your purpose—understanding why you're doing what you do will help you not give up or undermine/undervalue the process. Through the difficulty, resistance, and perseverance/tenacity, we're able to create the desired result.

What does this imply? When I walked into that basic fitness suite, my understanding of fitness and its benefits placed on me the demand and responsibility to use what is fundamental and create a maximum result. So stay on your end for the results.

Conclusively,

Abraham went through lots of pulls. After several years of not having a child, God again tested him by requesting his promised child. This he did without much complaint. If we don't learn to trust God completely, we will not exercise our full potential on earth. We must remain steadfast in the presence of God. We must hold onto His word for our breakthrough and turnaround. Be connected to God and the community of believers around you, and watch how well you will grow.

IRRESISTIBLE SOUND

Suppose you can see how comfortable I am in my shed. If I show you my shed, you will laugh. I want to redecorate my shed and convert it into a studio with sofas and various necessary equipment to make it an office.

Now, I'm visualizing. I'm not seeing all this rubbish. I see my sofa, my table, and my television. I see all the cameras. I know that it is coming to a time when it doesn't matter where I live, it doesn't matter how small I look on the outside, that the world won't be able to resist my sound, including queens, kings and the people in leadership positions.

They will not be able to resist my sound because out of me will come an incredible sound that will be heard beyond the shores of our nation.

Look, it depends on me allowing myself to be pulled by the Lord, and when I get pulled, I don't also determine when I get released.

That is the problem. We often get pulled, but we also want to select when we get released. You don't have control over the time for you to be released. You don't have control over the time for the kind of sound to be released.

The Bible said, "on time appointed." Until due time. God understands your due time, and I know everything will fall into place when my due time comes. My due time can be 2 hours from now. At any moment, Somebody in government just said they want to talk to you. They heard your voice somewhere, there is something you said, and they want to ask you a question."

From that moment, you strike a cord in that individual, and from that moment, they say, "are you available to come to the office of the prime minister at 10 am?" Yes! From that moment, are you available to chat with the prime minister? With just one conversation, everything changes. One meeting with the head of state, and you are assigned as a Special Adviser on Youth Development and Business

Affairs. From that moment, the world has known about you, your name.

It is why it doesn't matter how small a work God gives us; it doesn't matter how small he pulls or responds. What you're doing now may look insignificant but stay in position.

Have you ever asked yourself? Why am I involved in all these things I'm engaged in? One day, I wrote a list of all the different projects we were involved in and sent it to our administrative personnel. She was shocked. But what may seem like a lot to her is suited for me because of my pull.

Do you understand me? Because I have been given the grace for it, I do not see problems. What I see is the possibility of enhancing it. How can I be more efficient? How can I be effective? I see myself in a board meeting all the time with my twelve people working with me, having a meeting.

I can finish speaking in an important and high-profile meeting about the vision, and as excited as I am, I can still scrub the ground. It doesn't make any difference to me. Do you know why? Because my motivation comes from God, whose wealth and vastness cannot be defined. The one that called me has everything in his hands. He can command anybody anywhere right now, insert my name in their mind; they will call me up and tell me, Sir, I have just emailed, or I have just sent you a check for 1 million Dollars because my heart got moved. That is the God I serve, so why should I panic when I know that God is the one that can reward me if I allow myself to be pulled and to be released correctly?

QUESTIONS AND ANSWERS

QUESTION 1

Was Abraham pulled and released?

Considering Abraham's life, I don't pray for the pulling I see displayed in his life because it is clear that Abraham was pulled in several ways. This pull was manifest in his dedication to God. There is no debate that Abraham was blessed. However, this blessing did not extend to him having a child, which he would love to have.

There are people currently in a situation that epitomize what Abraham experienced. They have been faithful to God and very committed to the Lord, but they don't have a child. Medical experts have examined many, and there are no medically proven reasons why they should not have children. These people are being pulled in that area of life.

But children come from the Lord. They are part of God's blessings; they are the heritage of the Lord.

Being pulled can be very frustrating, especially if what you are experiencing contradicts your expectation.

Faith and total dependence on God are necessary during the pull because a lack of either can lead to questions in our minds.

The most common question I have heard from some is, when will I be released?

I have heard somebody say, I don't mind the pull, but I want to know when the release would happen.

Here is an analogy to explain this phenomenon. When you pull the strings of a guitar, it appears to be a short distance and time. However, when you look at the distance travelled from the realm of the spirit, remember that a day with the Lord is like a thousand years and vice versa.

Consequently, the work of faith is found between the pull and the release. Our trust in the Lord and consistency are recognised between the pull and the release.

How can you truly determine the distance the guitar chord was being pulled from a spiritual perspective?

In the same way, how can you establish how Abraham was pulled when it came to childbearing?

Secondly, Abraham was pulled when God told him to go up the mountain to "sacrifice his boy". The Bible says God tested him, meaning God pulled him differently to produce a different sound. In contrast to when God first pulled him, saying to him leave your father's house to a land I will show you. I can imagine Abraham saying to God, what are you saying? Leave my father, my mum, my family? This is my family, and I love them! But God says to leave them to a land I will show you, basically a land that God has not even told Abraham.

How do you walk with the Lord when pulled without clarity of vision? How do you walk with the Lord? To make this clearer, here is an example, let's assume you are directing me from my house to the superstore. I can begin to plan and determine the distance between my house and the store, and I can calibrate, calculate and project the strength required to get there from my home; however if you pull me somewhere without telling me the precise location of where we are going. I will likely assume a short-distance trip and may not even dress appropriately for a long one.

Where are we going, Lord? Where are you leading me to? Tell me! Can you give me an indication?

But God wants us to trust and follow Him irrespective.

Our walk with God must be on the backdrop of faith.

We are reminded in Hebrews 11:6:

"But without faith, it is impossible to [walk with God and] please Him, for whoever comes [near] to God must [necessarily] believe that God exists and that He rewards

those who [earnestly and diligently] seek Him." [The Amplified Bible]

Always attempting to figure out every detail before obeying God's instruction does not show faith.

When following God's instructions, we don't have to comprehend; we must learn to comply.

Did God completely disclose to Jesus every detail of what His suffering will entail? He knew He was on the earth for a particular mission, but did He fully comprehend the gruesome nature of that suffering?

There were prophecies about His death, "he was bruised for our transgressions,...the punishment that brought us peace was upon him, they chastised him, but do you know that there was no definite description of how graphic his pain would be? The piercing of His side, the crown of thorns, the denial of His friends, He had an idea of certain things, but He did not understand the full nature of the suffering.

If not, Jesus would not be telling God, "let this cup pass away." So yes, Abraham was pulled when he left his father's house. I don't think he danced and celebrated while leaving his family. Because of sentiments, Abraham must have struggled with the idea of leaving, remembering the good times, the family meals, and the disagreements that make family discussions even more enjoyable. The family birthday parties and fellowshipping together. And then you ask him to pack up and leave? To a place you haven't clearly described, defined and designed for him to see, evaluate and appreciate? For real?

It is easy to be critical of other people's pain without knowing what it feels like for them.

Every pain, every challenge, and every pull from God is uniquely designed for us. No two pull is the same.

We like the idea of **'by His wounds, we are healed'**, but do we care to identify the pain that preceded that?

Do we care to identify with the pain level that produces the amount of power we enjoy?

Can we relate to the pain associated with our peace?

1 Who has believed what he has heard from us?

   And to whom has the arm of the Lord been revealed?

2 For he grew up before him like a young plant,

   and like a root out of dry ground;

he had no form or majesty that we should look at him,

   and no beauty that we should desire him.

3 He was despised and rejected by men,

   a man of sorrows and acquainted with grief;

and as one from whom men hide their faces[f]

   he was despised, and we esteemed him not.

4 Surely he has borne our griefs

   and carried our sorrows;

yet we esteemed him stricken,

smitten by God, and afflicted.

5 But he was pierced for our transgressions;

he was crushed for our iniquities;

upon him was the chastisement that brought us peace,

and with his wounds we are healed.

[Isaiah 53:1-5 - English Standard Version]

Can I surprise you? People don't really pay attention to your pain if they can enjoy your power.

For those who have people depending on them for provision, protection and care, has any of your beneficiaries requested to sit with you and try to understand the level of pain you have been through in life to be able to have the amount of success you have now which allows you to provide for them?

Did they ever tell you to stop providing for them, except you elaborately describe how much suffering, studying, and sacrifice you had to experience to be this successful?

On the flip side, it would be best if you do not deprive anyone of enjoying the benefit of your experience, no matter how painful it was, because they can't identify with it.

There is a reason you had to survive that pain, that pressure, and that pull, which suggests that the pain was not designed to kill you.

Thank God you're still here.

Another way Abraham God pulled was when he separated from Lot, his nephew, because of increased wealth and a quarrel between their workers.

I have a nephew whom I love dearly, and I've been with him all his life. I can imagine if I must cut ties with him suddenly and move to a different place. That'll bring some pin with it.

Abraham had to let Lot choose where he went first.

God tested Abraham for his ability to let go, his detachment from material things and his capacity to handle more.

14 The LORD said to Abram after Lot had parted from him, "Look around from where you are, to the north and south, to the east and west.

15 All the land that you see I will give to you and your offspring[j] forever.

16 I will make your offspring like the dust of the earth, so that if anyone could count the dust, then your offspring could be counted.

17 Go, walk through the length and breadth of the land, for I am giving it to you."

18 So Abram went to live near the great trees of Mamre at Hebron, where he pitched his tents. There he built an altar to the LORD.

- Genesis 13:14-18 [New International Version]

The conversation between God and Abraham suggests that the pull was not for Lot but for Abraham.

God showed His involvement and declared blessings on Abraham after he allowed Lot to choose first.

God doesn't have to balance anything when He pulls you. He doesn't have to speak with all the parties involved when He gives you the assignment to do something, go somewhere or be with someone. Just comply! The pull is on you.

So, Abraham went through that. He went through lots of pulls. Then he went through the pull of not having a child. Then he went through the pull to sacrifice his son, the child of promise.

That is the height of pain. I mean, come on, now I have the boy, you say sacrifice him?

Abraham went through that, but for the Lord.

But before Abraham could literally sacrifice His son, a substitute was provided.

We must understand this, Abraham's obedience was not dependent on the promise of a replacement. He obeyed God whether there was a substitute or not.

Concerning Abraham and the promises of God for him, he was described as being fully persuaded or convinced that God was able to do what He had promised.

17 By faith Abraham, when he was put to the test [while the testing of his faith was still in progress], had already brought Isaac for an offering; he who had gladly received and welcomed [God's] promises was ready to sacrifice his only son,

18 Of whom it was said, Through Isaac shall your descendants be reckoned.

19 For he reasoned that God was able to raise [him] up even from among the dead. Indeed in the sense that Isaac was figuratively dead [potentially sacrificed], he did [actually]

receive him back from the dead.

- **Hebrews 11:17-19 [Amplified Bible, Classis Edition]**

QUESTION 2

Can you force a release?

A painful process can cause a self-initiated release from God's pull. Another reason an individual will force a premature release is by focusing too much on other people's sounds.

Some have tried to gain relevance through other means while competing with others whose release is due.

We have to understand this; we cannot help God.

David was anointed as King by the prophet Samuel, but he never forced the process. He never paraded himself as King until the appointed time, and the right opportunity presented itself.

He must have endured the pressure of knowing he is King but serving like someone of insignificance.

Like David, can you serve in a seemingly insignificant place or capacity even when you know that a renowned prophet like Samuel has anointed you as king?

Can you allow God to hide you despite public validation from a famous church leader or political or business leader? Would you comply with God's directives or force a release because you know you're anointed?

One might say to themselves I carry something inside of me, and people need to hear the sound now. The real question is, is it time for that sound to be released?

Of course, you carry something. You are undoubtedly loaded with these gifts and ideas, but is it time for people to hear them? In a concert, when you have an orchestra and the keyboard is performing an introductory piece, if the guitarist suddenly starts to strike the chords of the guitar out of time because he has something to play, he wants to be heard, it will lead to a distortion of the piece, and cause a mess.

Whenever we try to beat the release, we mess up the purpose for which we should be released. Whenever we try to beat the timing of the release, instead of blessing people, we send a polluted sound, a wrong sound. You don't have to be sinful to release the wrong sound or to be released wrongly. Missing the timings of God can cause the releasing of the wrong sound, especially when you don't listen to the Spirit of God; it is guaranteed for a wrong sound to be released when you don't listen or pay attention to the Spirit of God for your release.

If I get a directive from God to release a sound in 2021, and the people around me are prepared to that effect. However, suddenly there is an update not to release the sound till 2022. No matter how ready everyone has been, I will release that sound at the appointed time the Lord gave me. I will obey the Lord rather than attempt to please men because of sentiments. Because the message's relevance may not be felt in that year or is unnecessary because someone else has implemented something similar.

Attempting to force that release will only make me an echo. God's plan is for us to produce a unique sound and not an echo of an already existing sound.

Staying in rhythm with the timing of God's pull can only be facilitated by relying on the Holy Ghost.

Another example from scripture is John the Baptist and Jesus.

It could have been easy for Jesus to function like John the Baptist because he baptized and testified of him.

But Jesus didn't. His assignment was not to echo John the Baptist's ministry. His mandate was different, and so was His method of implementation.

Refrain from allowing anyone to force you into releasing a sound that is not due yet. Wait! There is timing to everything, even when it's too good to miss.

People's perception of what you can do, the uniqueness of your gift and the relevance of your voice should not put you under any pressure to perform. Walk in the spirit and know God's timing for your life.

Sometimes we have to decline politely,

Because it's an opportunity they say everyone is praying for doesn't qualify it to be yours.

The release of your sound is not just for people to be pleased by you; God must be pleased.

QUESTION 3

With the example of Jonah disobeying God, did Jonah resist being released by God after being pulled?

Absolutely, Jonah got pulled and resisted. He wanted to go where he wanted. God wanted Nineveh, and he wanted Tarshish. God sent him to a land to preach repentance; he wanted a land where he could trade in business.

But God doesn't send us to where we want. He doesn't pull us comfortably. God's pull is not *just the way we like it*. His pull is designed and configured for us according to His divine will.

So, Jonah had an idea of where he wanted to go, but God's pull gave a different signal.

If he goes to Tarshish, he could transact business; he may employ people, become influential politically, and become a blessing to people through his enterprise, but is it pleasing to God?

The question is, have you carried out a sound check?

Are you where you ought to be and to do what you should do?

Is God pleased with your sound? Have you become comfortable because people applaud you?

It's time for a SOUND CHECK.

1 Now the word of the Lord came to Jonah son of Amittai, saying,

2 Arise, go to Nineveh, that great city, and proclaim against it, for their wickedness has come up before Me.

3 But Jonah rose up to flee to Tarshish from being in the presence of the Lord [as His prophet] and went down to Joppa and found a ship going to Tarshish [the most remote of the Phoenician trading places then known]. So he paid the appointed fare and went down into the ship to go with them to Tarshish from being in the presence of the Lord [as His servant and minister].

4 But the Lord sent out a great wind upon the sea, and there was a violent tempest on the sea so that the ship was about to be broken.

- Jonah 1:1-4 [Amplified Bible, Classic Edition]

QUESTION 4

What are the things that prevent people from recognizing they are being pulled?

Discomfort is one of the significant reasons many don't recognize the pull of God. Many who have grown up in the church are trained to believe anything negative is the devil. So, when God pulls them, they don't see the signal, for it appears to them as the devil attacking them.

Therefore, they try to bind God's will because they are neither sensitive to him nor understand the mind of God. Also, they don't understand what God is doing due to how they have been cultured and the old paradigm and habitual ways of thinking. So, if something contrary happens, the devil is at work, and they resist.

Some have resisted the pull because of ignorance. They resisted instead of responding because it was uncomfortable.

Part of the definition of being pulled by force is that it can be discomforting. It takes you away from your comfort zone. It takes you away from familiarity, and it takes you away from what you like to do and the people you want.

The human mind responds to pain as unfavourable but it's not entirely correct.

In the book of Exodus, we read how God deployed a painful and lengthy journey to preserve the Israelites for the promise He kept for them.

17 It so happened that after Pharaoh released the people, God didn't lead them by the road through the land of the Philistines, which was the shortest route, for God thought, "If the people encounter war, they'll change their minds and go back to Egypt."

18 So God led the people on the wilderness road, looping around to the Red Sea. The Israelites left Egypt in military formation.

- Exodus 13:17-18 [The Message Translation]

God is the master planner. Because of the opposition in the short route, he took them through a more comprehensive course so they would not change their mind and return to Egypt.

Your journey is longer doesn't mean God is not involved.

The process is demanding doesn't mean God is not involved.

Doors are shut at you doesn't mean it was not authorised by God.

Encountering a significant amount of opposition or setback doesn't mean God is not involved.

We must understand that the master planner, God, is not preparing the promise. The promise is designed and set; instead, our mind is undergoing a configuration process to match what has already been prepared. That's the reason for the discomfort.

128

QUESTION 5

What hinders the release from happening in the lives of individuals?

One thing that hinders people is they want to understand the pull and dictate the sound. Let's look at the ministry, for example, If God releases you into children's ministry but your idea of ministry has always been leading a congregation immediately. You will have a reluctant approach and response to that release.

But as we mentioned earlier in the book, every release initiates a new pull.

There is no moment when the pull becomes over. There will always be a pull if we must stay relevant in our area of calling and assignment.

The key here is to yield. Total surrender to the will of God. The apostle Paul has a better way of putting this;

30 [For that matter], why do I live [dangerously as I do, running such risks that I am] in peril every hour?

31 [I assure you] by the pride which I have in you in [your fellowship and union with] Christ Jesus our Lord, that I die daily [I face death every day and die to self].

32 What do I gain if, merely from the human point of view, I fought with [wild] beasts at Ephesus? If the dead are not raised [at all], let us eat and drink, for tomorrow we will be dead.

- 1 Corinthians 15:30-33 [Amplified Bible, Classic Edition]

Let's take it to a business example; The day that God wants to release you in the business sector, on that day, you are supposed to do a short presentation to the janitors; to speak to the cleaners, but that is not what you've envisaged at your release.

You visualised the release with a board of directors, with the top bosses.

So, because of preconceived ideas of what our release should be, we often miss out on the release.

A preconceived notion could be that presenting to janitors does not bring me relevance and prominence, but my promotion will come quickly if I present to CEOs and top bosses.

Let's paint a picture:

You find yourself with the opportunity to train the janitors and make a presentation to them. During this session, something you said might have caught their attention, and they joked about it because of their limited knowledge of a technical term used. While joking in the company's cafeteria during lunch, they mentioned the word 'cybernetics', which you used during your training session, and one of the technical bosses heard them.

131

The CEO might stop them and say who said cybernetics? Then they come to call you to see what more you know, as one thing leads to the other, they are offering you a job because this is what they have been looking for in their company, a person with insight into cybernetics.

Many are waiting for an opportunity with captains of the industry while refusing to captain the little they have been assigned.

10 "If you are faithful in little things, you will be faithful in large ones. But if you are dishonest in little things, you won't be honest with greater responsibilities.

-   Luke 16:10 [New Living Translation]

QUESTION 6

Could a person miss a release that has already occurred?

Completely yes. John the Baptist was anticipating the coming of the king and new kingdom while Jesus was already here.

Because the release doesn't fit into your paradigm doesn't make it less of a release.

1 After Jesus had finished instructing his twelve disciples, he went on from there to teach and preach in the towns of Galilee.

2 When John, who was in prison, heard about the deeds of the Messiah, he sent his disciples

3 to ask him, "Are you the one who is to come, or should we expect someone else?"

4 Jesus replied, "Go back and report to John what you hear and see:

5 The blind receive sight, the lame walk, those who have leprosy are cleansed, the deaf hear, the dead are raised, and the good news is proclaimed to the poor.

6 Blessed is anyone who does not stumble on account of me."

- Matthew 11;1-6 [New International Version]

What you expect may be with you now, but you will only receive it if it is perceived correctly. This implies that it is very easy to miss a release because of perception problems.

More recently, I've been praying to God for awareness and consciousness because many things we've been asking God for are around us, but because we look in the wrong place, we're not seeing what God has already given.

Elisha and his servant had supernatural protection at their disposal, but because of the lack of revelation on the side of his servant, he panicked.

When Elisha prayed that God should open his servant's eyes, he was only praying for the conscious awareness of his servant to realise what was already there. Having our eyes opened spiritually, and enlightened enables us to recognise the release.

15 When the servant of the man of God got up and went out early the next morning, an army with horses and chariots had surrounded the city. "Oh no, my lord! What shall we do?" the servant asked.

16 "Don't be afraid," the prophet answered. "Those who are with us are more than those who are with them."

17 And Elisha prayed, "Open his eyes, Lord, so that he may see." Then the Lord opened the servant's eyes, and he looked and saw the hills full of horses and chariots of fire all around Elisha.

- 2 Kings 6:15-17 [New International Version]

Apostle Paul prayed that we have the Spirit of wisdom and Revelation in the knowledge of Him and that the eyes of our understanding be enlightened so that we may know the hope of our calling.

15-19 That's why, when I heard of the solid trust you have in the Master Jesus and your outpouring of love to all the followers of Jesus, I couldn't stop thanking God for you— every time I prayed, I'd think of you and give thanks. But I do more than thank. I ask—ask the God of our Master, Jesus Christ, the God of glory—to make you intelligent and discerning in knowing him personally, your eyes focused and clear, so that you can see exactly what it is he is calling you to do, grasp the immensity of this glorious way of life he has for his followers, oh, the utter extravagance of his work in us who trust him—endless energy, boundless strength!

- Ephesians 1:15-17 [The message Translation]

An acknowledgement of the existence of a thing cannot be mistaken for the creation of that thing. It is already there; all you need is a revelation to find it out.

What can you see?

QUESTION 7

Does waiting on God play any role in being pulled and released?

There's long-suffering because, as I said, you don't determine when the release comes.

You don't determine it. It can be painful. I have been in that place.

A person's idea of your release time should never unsettle you while you're still in the process.

People conceive different ideas on how your release should be or where your release should be, or when your release should be, but you must be very sensitive to the voice of the Lord. You must understand what God is saying to you.

You must know when to be released; otherwise, out of excitement, out of pressure, out of people compelling you, out of the need people place on you, it can move you into releasing what God has given you prematurely.

138

When Jesus and the disciples went to the Mount of Transfiguration, you know, Jesus pulled them into the Mount of Transfiguration, away from the rest of the group. He instructed them not to disclose what they encountered until the appointed time.

It appears conflicting for Jesus to instruct them not to share their great encounter. But there is a need for the understanding of timing.

1 And after six days Jesus took with him Peter and James, and John his brother, and led them up a high mountain by themselves. 2 And he was transfigured before them, and his face shone like the sun, and his clothes became white as light.

3 And behold, there appeared to them Moses and Elijah, talking with him.

4 And Peter said to Jesus, "Lord, it is good that we are here. If you wish, I will make three tents here, one for you and one for Moses and one for Elijah."

5 He was still speaking when, behold, a bright cloud overshadowed them, and a voice from the cloud said, "This is my beloved Son, with whom I am well pleased; listen to him."

6 When the disciples heard this, they fell on their faces and were terrified.

7 But Jesus came and touched them, saying, "Rise, and have no fear."

8 And when they lifted up their eyes, they saw no one but Jesus only.

9 And as they were coming down the mountain, Jesus commanded them, "Tell no one the vision, until the Son of Man is raised from the dead."

Matthew 17:1-9 [English Standard Version]

Sometimes you have to wait. You can't disclose everything at every time to everyone.

We must be very sensitive, discerning, and understanding of what the Spirit of God says regarding the release.

Even the movie industry understands the need for release dates. They don't just throw everything out there because it sounds and look attractive. They discern the season before releasing a movie.

Waiting on God before the release is very personal to me. I know what it feels like to move from a place of significance to an unfamiliar place and be left in the dark.

I know what it feels like to leave one place of recognition and be positioned in another place to undertake menial jobs as part of the waiting process. There was no timeline, no explanation, and no expectation. All I had was my faith and my surrender; during this period, I ran errands like that's all I was in this life to do. And I did all this with joy and dignity. This period stretched and tested me but taught me and prepared me for today. This was my training ground. It was my school of ministry. This was my school of leadership and diplomatic studies. But, of course, I only discovered all I had learned in hindsight. I never completely grasped all this while in the process; I only obeyed.

I was loved, disciplined, corrected, and sometimes very openly and painfully because I often flunked, missed deadlines, and made the wrong calls. But thank God I had an excellent teacher in my pastor.

Compared to the standard this new church organisation was operating on, I was presented very uncut to my pastor, but he was willing, caring and loving to work with me. He saw what even I couldn't see. This is why he pushed me and placed demands on me that I felt uncomfortable with and sometimes incompetent to implement.

But during that period, I was conditioned to be result oriented, resourceful and creative.

Not only was I pulled into position, but God used my pastor to pull every negative mindset out of me.

But that is where I learnt this statement.

'Excuses are tools of incompetence, monuments of nothingness, and those who use them are not wise.'

I encourage you to pause now and then and appreciate the people God used and is still using in your waiting process. People who place a demand on you because of what God installed in you. Things you couldn't even see in yourself. Such people are a rare find.

Check this out; it is very easy to desire to lead a nation, a group of people, or a major corporation. But just like David, can God trust you with a few sheep and goats behind the scenes where you're not visibly acknowledged?

Can you serve away from the stage?

Can you serve behind the scenes where you are not seen?

143

Can you actively and effectively be a significant part of a seemingly insignificant vision? Or a tiny, minuscule part of an extensive organisation? A dot in the entire sentence? Responses to these questions will determine the state of your mind for a release.

QUESTION 8

Can the devil imitate a pull from God?

Yes, the devil can imitate a pull and a release.

An endorsement of your gift is not necessarily the sign of a God-ordained release.

An affirmation from man is not necessarily an approval from God. It may be a set-up from the devil.

Today, where many are desperate for validation, affirmation and acknowledgement, we must discern what spirit is speaking the right words.

The words spoken are correct doesn't necessarily validate the source.

16 As we were going to the place of prayer, we were met by a slave girl who had a spirit of divination and brought her owners much gain by fortune-telling.

17 She followed Paul and us, crying out, "These men are servants of the Most High God, who proclaim to you the way of salvation."

18 And this she kept doing for many days. Paul, having become greatly annoyed, turned and said to the spirit, "I command you in the name of Jesus Christ to come out of her." And it came out that very hour.

Acts 16:16-18 [English Standard Version]

Paul and the others were silent for a while, perhaps processing what was happening, but after a couple of days, Paul got upset because he knew that was not the Spirit of God speaking. He rebuked the woman and cast the Devil out of her because even though her proclamation should cause them to be noticed and listened to, it looked like a release that should make the people believe in them, but it wasn't from God. That was not a release. It was a set-up for destruction, to invalidate their ministry, and eventually bring them to disrepute while making money for the perpetrators.

This lady was making a profit for her masters. So, we must be mindful of this; because people announce you do not mean it is your release.

You must be very careful because people invite you to their platform, announce your name, love on you, tell people about you, promote your work, advertise you, and share every of your social media posts does not mean it's motivated by the spirit of God.

Not every good deed is a God deed.

We have mentioned training, pain and other adverse situations in this book, and some may conclude that every challenging problem they encounter must be God pulling them. That's not correct.

Let us compare these texts.

1 Corinthians 12:1-9 [English Standard Version]

1 I must go on boasting. Though there is nothing to be gained by it, I will go on to visions and revelations of the Lord.

147

2 I know a man in Christ who fourteen years ago was caught up to the third heaven—whether in the body or out of the body I do not know, God knows.

3 And I know that this man was caught up into paradise—whether in the body or out of the body I do not know, God knows—

4 and he heard things that cannot be told, which man may not utter.

5 On behalf of this man I will boast, but on my own behalf I will not boast, except of my weaknesses—

6 though if I should wish to boast, I would not be a fool, for I would be speaking the truth; but I refrain from it, so that no one may think more of me than he sees in me or hears from me.

7 So to keep me from becoming conceited because of the surpassing greatness of the revelations, a thorn was given me in the flesh, a messenger of Satan to harass me, to keep me from becoming conceited.

8 Three times I pleaded with the Lord about this, that it should leave me.

9 But he said to me, "My grace is sufficient for you, for my power is made perfect in weakness." Therefore I will boast all the more gladly of my weaknesses, so that the power of Christ may rest upon me.

10 For the sake of Christ, then, I am content with weaknesses, insults, hardships, persecutions, and calamities. For when I am weak, then I am strong.

Acts 28:1-6 [English Standard Version]

1 After we were brought safely through, we then learned that the island was called Malta.

2 The native people showed us unusual kindness, for they kindled a fire and welcomed us all, because it had begun to rain and was cold.

3 When Paul had gathered a bundle of sticks and put them on the fire, a viper came out because of the heat and fastened on his hand.

4 When the native people saw the creature hanging from his hand, they said to one another, "No doubt this man is a murderer. Though he has escaped from the sea, Justice has not allowed him to live."

5 He, however, shook off the creature into the fire and suffered no harm.

6 They were waiting for him to swell up or suddenly fall down dead. But when they had waited a long time and saw no misfortune come to him, they changed their minds and said that he was a god.

Firstly, there is a purpose to every pull.

In 1 Corinthians 12, we see that the purpose of Paul's affliction was to keep him from *becoming conceited or excessively proud of himself because of the surpassing greatness of the revelations he saw.* Consequently, he prayed to God 3 times to take the pain away, but God didn't. God instead released grace to him. Paul was given the ability to withstand the pain. God did not take the pain away, but pride was taken out of him through that affliction.

Often we pray for a God to take us away from a particular situation, but God's intention may be to take something out of us through that situation.

But we cannot confuse 1 Corinthians 12 for Acts 28; hence Paul did not pray for the snake to be taken away; he shook the snake into the fire.

We must be sensitive to identify what to pray about and what to shake into the fire. Not every affliction is a pull.

1 Kings 13:9-32 – [New King James Version]

[9] For so it was commanded me by the word of the LORD, saying, 'You shall not eat bread, nor drink water, nor return by the same way you came.'

[10] So he went another way and did not return by the way he came to Bethel.

¹¹ Now an old prophet dwelt in Bethel, and his sons came and told him all the works that the man of God had done that day in Bethel; they also told their father the words which he had spoken to the king.

¹² And their father said to them, "Which way did he go?" For his sons had seen which way the man of God went who came from Judah.

¹³ Then he said to his sons, "Saddle the donkey for me." So, they saddled the donkey for him; and he rode on it,

¹⁴ and went after the man of God, and found him sitting under an oak. Then he said to him, "*Are* you the man of God who came from Judah?"

And he said, "I *am.*"

¹⁵ Then he said to him, "Come home with me and eat bread."

¹⁶ And he said, "I cannot return with you nor go in with you; neither can I eat bread nor drink water with you in this place.

¹⁷ For I have been told by the word of the LORD, 'You shall not eat bread nor drink water there, nor return by going the way you came.' "

[18] He said to him, "I too *am* a prophet as you *are,* and an angel spoke to me by the word of the LORD, saying, 'Bring him back with you to your house, that he may eat bread and drink water.'" (He was lying to him.)

[19] So he went back with him, and ate bread in his house, and drank water.

[20] Now it happened, as they sat at the table, that the word of the LORD came to the prophet who had brought him back;

[21] and he cried out to the man of God who came from Judah, saying, "Thus says the LORD: 'Because you have disobeyed the word of the LORD, and have not kept the commandment which the LORD your God commanded you,

[22] but you came back, ate bread, and drank water in the place of which *the LORD* said to you, "Eat no bread and drink no water," your corpse shall not come to the tomb of your fathers.' "

[23] So it was, after he had eaten bread and after he had drunk, that he saddled the donkey for him, the prophet whom he had brought back.

[24] When he was gone, a lion met him on the road and killed him. And his corpse was thrown on the road, and the donkey stood by it. The lion also stood by the corpse.

[25] And there, men passed by and saw the corpse thrown on the road, and the lion standing by the corpse. Then they went and told *it* in the city where the old prophet dwelt.

[26] Now when the prophet who had brought him back from the way heard *it,* he said, "It *is* the man of God who was disobedient to the word of the LORD. Therefore, the LORD has delivered him to the lion, which has torn him and killed him, according to the word of the LORD which He spoke to him."

[27] And he spoke to his sons, saying, "Saddle the donkey for me." So, they saddled *it.*

[28] Then he went and found his corpse thrown on the road, and the donkey and the lion standing by the corpse. The lion had not eaten the corpse nor torn the donkey.

29 And the prophet took up the corpse of the man of God, laid it on the donkey, and brought it back. So, the old prophet came to the city to mourn, and to bury him.

30 Then he laid the corpse in his own tomb; and they mourned over him, *saying,* "Alas, my brother!"

31 So it was, after he had buried him, that he spoke to his sons, saying, "When I am dead, then bury me in the tomb where the man of God *is* buried; lay my bones beside his bones.

32 For the saying which he cried out by the word of the LORD against the altar in Bethel, and against all the shrines on the high places which *are* in the cities of Samaria, will surely come to pass."

The above verse is an example of a wrong pull.

Mainly for this generation, that example is a good one.

You may have had this experience as I have of people telling you what they saw in a vision and what an angel said to them in their dream. But scrutinize everything under the microscope of God's word.

This was the statement that entrapped the young prophet;

18 And he said to him, "I also am a prophet as you are, and an angel spoke to me by the word of the Lord, saying, 'Bring him back with you into your house that he may eat bread and drink water.' But he lied to him.

It was an endorsement by an older prophet, identifying himself in a similar office as the young prophet. Which ordinarily could get any young minister excited.

But what makes you think that because they bear the title and speak the language, they're saying the mind of God?

Some validation is only an attempt to bring destruction.

Some stages are not set up for your elevation. They're not set up to celebrate you but to castrate you. Their motive is to deprive you of power, vitality, and vigour.

These people and places are not there to elevate you but to emasculate you.

Some people saw something in their dream but was it from God? Very often, out of our desire, excitement, or what we want, we can visualize, dream something, and then think it's from God. It may not be from God.

In 2 Peter 2:1-3, the New King James Version, the bible warns us to stay alert:

But there were also false prophets among the people, even as there will be false teachers among you, who will secretly bring in destructive heresies, even denying the Lord who bought them, and bring on themselves swift destruction.

² And many will follow their destructive ways, because of whom the way of truth will be blasphemed.

³ By covetousness they will exploit you with deceptive words; for a long time their judgment has not been idle, and their destruction [a]does not slumber.

Summary

One big lesson I learnt during my processes and continue to learn is that the pull is individualised and unique to you and me. But the release is not limited to you alone; its reach and impact are far beyond you.

As you surrender to the pull and posture yourself for the release, these are my declarations over you:

Isaiah 60:1-7 [Amplified Bible, Classic Edition]

61Arise [from the depression and prostration in which circumstances have kept you—rise to a new life]! Shine (be radiant with the glory of the Lord), for your light has come, and the glory of the Lord has risen upon you!

2 For behold, darkness shall cover the earth, and dense darkness [all] peoples, but the Lord shall arise upon you [O Jerusalem], and His glory shall be seen on you.

3 And nations shall come to your light, and kings to the brightness of your rising.

4 Lift up your eyes round about you and see! They all gather themselves together, they come to you. Your sons shall come from afar, and your daughters shall be carried and nursed in the arms.

5 Then you shall see and be radiant, and your heart shall thrill and tremble with joy [at the glorious deliverance] and be enlarged; because the abundant wealth of the [Dead] Sea shall be turned to you, unto you shall the nations come with their treasures.

6 A multitude of camels [from the eastern trading tribes] shall cover you [Jerusalem], the young camels of Midian and Ephah; all the men from Sheba [who once came to trade] shall come, bringing gold and frankincense and proclaiming the praises of the Lord.

7 All the flocks of Kedar shall be gathered to you [as the eastern pastoral tribes join the trading tribes], the rams of Nebaioth shall minister to you; they shall come up with acceptance on My altar, and My glorious house I will glorify.

God will pull us to places where we think we have decided to do certain things, but it's a release.

God's pull is not necessarily painful. It doesn't always have to be painful. The pain doesn't have to be something destructive.

A decision you suddenly make to relocate may be a pull from God.

The word pull means to move something towards yourself, while another definition says to take something out of or away from a place, especially using physical effort.

So, God might pull you towards Himself or a place or a person, and at other times, God can pull you out of something, somewhere or from someone.

But the purpose is to release a unique sound.

The Bible, according to Matthew 4:1, records that:

"Then Jesus was led up by the Spirit into the wilderness to be tempted by the devil."

Jesus was pulled into the wilderness at a very vulnerable time after fasting for forty days for the purpose of being tempted, tested, and tried.

There is always a purpose to the pull.

PULLED AND RELEASED

GLOSSARY OF TERMS

Definition

To pull is to cause movement of something or someone towards oneself either forcefully or steadily. To release is to allow something to move, act or flow freely…enable escape / set free.

Natural Context

A guitar makes no sound if it's not released; the string of a guitar does not determine the sound, but the way it's PULLED determines the sound that comes forth. It is the player that determines / controls the sound…not the instrument.

Question – who is in control of your life…are you pulling the strings or someone else?

A harp can only make noise if the strings are pulled and then released.

An arrow can only be released, if it's pulled backwards.

162

Spiritual Context

- To pull something requires effort...it requires taking a step backwards. Hence, many people desire to be RELEASED, yet they don't want to be PULLED.

- To be RELEASED, you first need to be PULLED.

- Many people resist and wrestle against being PULLED, because to be PULLED comes with consequences.

- The main requirement associated with being PULLED is SURRENDER...having to die to self and submit to God.

- In the arena of being PULLED...you begin to know the real you.

- In the PULLED arena, it's important to visualise the RELEASE and walk towards it.

- God has put a sound on the inside of us...when a note has been released, your Spirit hears and responds.

- Too many people have been singing...yet no-one hears their notes because it's not Holy Spirit led. When you are led by the Holy Spirit, your sound will be heard.

163

- When God (not self) releases you, you produce a different sound in the realm of the Spirit.

- No one knows the time of their RELEASE; rest assured, if God has PULLED you, you will be RELEASED at the right time (Ecclesiastes 3:1-8).

- A RELEASE that takes place out of time REDUCES, it BLOCKS…wait on God for the right time.

- It's imperative to allow yourself, led by Holy Spirit, to be RELASED correctly.

Biblical Context

1. Joshua

Joshua 9 Verse 14 says 'they did not consult the Lord'

It makes it clear that one of the ways we can easily be pulled wrongly or deceitfully is when we don't consult the Lord. Being distant from the Lord makes us susceptible to deception, manipulation and confusion.

Read: Joshua 9:1-15

We must be very sensitive because these people came to Joshua and the Israelites, pretending to be in a vulnerable position. They disguised themselves and placed demands like people who need help, but it was an entrapment, their intentions were wrong.

Be careful and very discerning in identifying what God has presented as those in need.

Because someone appears vulnerable does not mean that you open yourself and your matters immediately to them. The people in the text gathered intel on Joshua and his people. They recounted what the Lord had done for the Israelites against the other nations. They had very detailed information of the blessings of the Lord on Joshua and his people.

I mean, I would get excited if people come from a far country and start talking about what the Lord has done through me and for me.

But the question is, what is their motive?

Why are they telling me all that?

What do they really want?

We must place our ears close to the mouth of God to listen; and our mouths close to His ears to consult with and enquire from Him.

2. Jesus

Jesus died a painful death that stretched His will – Luke 22:42

He understood that in order to produce many seeds (save humanity and restore us back to the original plan), He needed to die (PULLED) and then rise (RELEASED).

John 12: 24 Very truly I tell you, unless a kernel of wheat falls to the ground and dies, it remains only a single seed. But if it dies, it produces many seeds.

3. Disciples

The disciples were PULLED (had to surrender and be trained in their calling) and then RELEASED (became Apostles). Read Matthew 16:24, Acts 2:4.

4.Abraham

Abraham was PULLED (tested to sacrifice Isaac) then RELEASED (through his offspring, all nations on earth were blessed). Read Genesis 22.

5. Paul and Silas

Paul and Silas were PULLED (arrested and put in prison) and RELEASED (they were released by God and saved several souls). Read Acts 16:16-40.

6. Ruth

Ruth was PULLED to follow Naomi, after her painful experiences (to live in Bethlehem) and then RELEASED (married Boaz). Read Ruth 1:16-18 and Ruth 4.

7. David

David was PULLED (to fight Goliath) and RELEASED (became King).

Sometimes once RELEASED, it can take years to be established.

(It took David several years after his anointing to become King).

Different Type of Pulls

- Word for thought: you can be PULLED in different directions on purpose for a purpose. When you are PULLED in different directions, you make different / unique sounds.

- To survive being PULLED...requires SURRENDER, TRUST and OBEDIENCE.

- It is important to obey God against popular opinion.

- If God PULLS you, it's important to be willing.

Jacob – wrestle with angel

Learning – if you PULL by your own strength, there are consequences. Read Genesis 32:22-31

The pull is always individualised. It's unique to you, but the release is not limited to you; its reach is beyond you. Before Jacob had his encounter, he was sensitive to being alone, and pulled away from his family, the people he loved.

Jesus – tempted by Satan.

Learning – when you are PULLED correctly, you will reap blessings in your RELEASE. Read Matt 4: 1-11

Abraham – pulled in several directions

Learning - no matter how many times Abraham was PULLED, he trusted and obeyed God e.g. PULLED to leave his land (Genesis 12), PULLED to sacrifice his son (Genesis 22) etc.

- How do you walk with God when being pulled in a direction you don't know?...it's important to trust God, obey, surrender and have faith.

Paul – pulled for a divine mission / assignment

Learning – Paul never resisted the PULL (blinded by light) and

169

upon his release, immediately got baptised and begun his missions. Read Acts 9:17-19.

What Hinders Releases

- Disobedience hinders your RELEASE, e.g., a journey that should have taken 40 days took 40 years for the Israelites.

- Some people get PULLED and they want to RELEASE themselves…they announce themselves quicker than they should. When this happens, God's hands are removed…flesh operates and no longer Spirit. God will only finish what He started.

- An 'out of time' RELEASE blocks and pollutes the sound. You will be seen but not heard by God in heaven. You will be heard in the natural, but the sound is contaminated and displeases God. - question…is God pleased by you?

- Lack of wisdom – Don't discuss your pull with everyone. Human emotions can talk you out of your RELEASE.

Jonah

Learning – he was PULLED but did not want to yield which led to disobedience.

Judas

Learning – he was PULLED, but he decided to RELEASE himself which led to his death / downfall...

John the Baptist

Learning – perception of the anointing can put a demand on you. Being sensitive to the Holy Spirit helps you to know the right time to release a sound.

How do you know if you are being PULLED?

- It takes you away from comfort.
- You will hear God's voice – Abraham was told to 'leave his land'.
- Surrender – required to submit to the will of God alone.

Quick Release vs. Short Release

Word for thought: Sometimes a RELEASE can initiate a PULL.

- David – after defeating Goliath, he waited several years to be king.

- Joseph – the journey from pit to the palace.

Other Notes

- Your RELEASE will announce you.

- A RELEASE can open a rhythm of blessings.

- Oppositions can come, but nothing will stop your RELEASE.

- Your RELEASE can come in the form of a problem (e.g. Goliath)

- If your eyes are spiritually open, you will identify your RELEASE.

- There is a time for your RELEASE…be patient.

- You don't determine when the RELEASE comes…trust God.

- Many things we have prayed for have been RELEASED in the Spirit already. ...being aware saves time.

- The closer you are to God, the easier the PULL; the further you are from God, the harder the PULL.

- When you have a close relationship with God, you will recognise the PULL and RELEASE.

- The deeper you are PULLED, the further you are RELEASED.

- The devil may imitate a RELEASE...discernment is needed, e.g., Paul and Silas.

- There are many people suffering due to wrong PULLS.

  Read 1 Kings 13 and 2 Peter 2:1-3.

Printed in Great Britain
by Amazon

19031566R00099